How to Make Money on Fiverr Secrets Revealed

How Using Fiverr Has Allowed Me to Quit My Job and
Work Only Four Hours a Week

James Chen

I0510085

Table of Contents

Making Money On Fiverr: The Basics

The #1 Rule for Fiverr Gigs

Money. We would all like more of it. And Fiverr is a fantastic resource for making money. A lot of money. But you have to be careful not to fall into an easy trap with Fiverr, which is undervaluing your time. Too often sellers start a gig that takes too much time to fulfill. Since you only make four dollars for each gig—with Fiverr taking the other dollar—it makes sense that your gig should not take you longer than ten minutes to complete. The shorter it takes, the better.

This rule is the most important thing to keep in mind when posting a gig. How long will it take me to do? Think about it this way: if it takes you ten minutes to complete a gig at 4 dollars per gig that is 24 dollars an hour. This should be your minimum rate. Now compare this with it taking a half hour to complete a gig. That will give you only $8 an hour. That's essentially a minimum wage job.

Let's take it a step further. Imagine you have an unlimited amount of gigs. If your ceiling is $8 per hour, no matter how hard you work, you are not going to break through. Your chances improve if you hit the $24 an hour mark, but even then you have to work constantly to make more money.

The Best Gigs

The point is that to make money on Fiverr, you can't post any type of gig; most will not make you money because you have to work too long and too hard. The best gigs are ones that can be completed easily or in which the information is complete and just needs to be sent to the buyer. In the past, I've had gigs that sold pdf documents to buyers that contained everything from recipes to dating information. It is great when it sells, but there was never much demand. While it is a good gig to have posted on Fiverr, it won't make you money. So just because you can do it quickly doesn't mean it will make you a lot of money. The demand has to be there, too.

These type of easy gigs without much demand are fine to keep up, just understand that they won't be your bread and butter. Some gigs seem easy, but can be actually quite time consuming. Video testimonials, audio transcription, singing or playing an instrument, and drawing or doing any kind of art takes way too much time and effort. Even if you are fantastic at these areas, you still need to invest the time to complete the order. And you want to be able to over-deliver on your gigs so you can get repeat customers; I don't see that happening with these types of gigs.

How to Really Make Money Using Fiverr

So this leaves us with the question: what is an acceptable gig? I will give you one type of gig that does well on Fiverr; it is actually easy to complete and has a high demand. But even that gig doesn't take advantage of Fiverr, using it to its fullest potential. In order to do that, you need to buyer and not a seller, and market your product to those outside of Fiverr. This sounds more complicated than it truly is. And I will go through it later in this guide. The reason it makes money is simple: you spend your time getting leads and customers, while a seller on Fiverr does all the work. And you end up charging much more than five dollars.

The beauty of Fiverr is using the sellers as outsourcers who are able to supply product for you. You then charge your customers much more. Think of it as being the middleman in the transaction. You buy the product on Fiverr for wholesale, and then turnaround and sell it for any price you wish; you dictate the market.

Does it work? Absolutely. The right products sell themselves. Even better, with these products it will be incredibly simple to target your audience.

Most books will tell you how to make money on Fiverr. This one will tell you how to make money using Fiverr. The difference—and potential profits—are huge.

What Makes Money on Fiverr

So we know that we want a gig that doesn't take much time to fulfill. As I mentioned earlier, sending pdf documents that cover various topics are great gigs. The demand isn't going to be high, though. So if we want to actually make a fair amount of money we need to focus on another type of gig.

Gig Extras

But first I want to talk about gig extras. These are extras you can charge customers on your gig when you become a Level 1 seller. Gig extras can definitely help you make more money from your gig. However, you never want to lose sight of how long it takes you to do the basic gig. If it is more than ten minutes, then gig extras still are not likely to help you supercharge your business. Because this book is more about using Fiverr than selling on Fiverr, gig extras will only be briefly mentioned. While they can be helpful to your bottom line, to really make money you are going to want to use Fiverr to outsource your work, while selling it for a much higher price.

Sneaky Tricks to Get Noticed

When you are first starting out on Fiverr, you won't get many views or orders for you gig. The way the system is it takes time to get orders. And complete orders and positive reviews are necessary to really see future orders. The good news is that if you are in the high-demand field I will tell you about, orders should eventually come your way after a few days. If you don't get an order within ten days, I would suggest deleting and re-posting your gig with slightly different wording.

Another suggestion is to have a friend buy your gig and post a positive review on it. This will greatly help, improving your visibility. Many customers won't even bother with your gig if you don't have at least one review, so getting that review as soon as possible is highly recommended.

Also, if you are having problems getting interest in your gig, email Fiverr asking if they can promote your gig. Fiverr support is excellent, and they have been very receptive to this in the past, so I highly recommend doing it. At the very worst, they say no, but it is always worth trying, because if they promote you, you will see a lot of orders.

Another way to get recognition quickly is to provide more than your competitors. It is a good idea to look at the gigs of your competitors, see what they are offering, and see which ones are having success. Then try to offer a little bit more. If you can highlight this difference in your gig title, even better; it will produce results. Once you have gotten a few reviews, and the orders start to pile up, you can edit your gig to be more in line with your competitors. Undercut them to get noticed, but once noticed you no longer should offer additional service.

When the orders do start to come in, make certain that you deliver them on time. Delivering orders late will have serious repercussions for your gig, so don't do it. With the gig I'll suggest this shouldn't be a problem, but understand that if you want to be successful on Fiverr you can never deliver late.

Be professional. You might be surprised at how many Fiverr sellers lack professionalism. You want to make certain that you are incredibly responsive to your potential customers; try to answer their questions as quickly as possible. Repeat customers will be your lifeblood, so you want to make sure you treat all your customers well so that they will come back. I always try to work within my customer's requirements as long as they don't violate my rule about a gig taking longer than ten minutes. Gigs that allow you to over-deliver on the product easily are great, leaving the customer believing that they got a fantastic deal. Leaving your customers happy is a great way to continue to make money with any Fiverr deal.

Start with this Money-Making Gig

That is enough of the preliminaries. I now want to look at the gig you want to set up on Fiverr. There is a huge market on Fiverr for reviewers. The most common ones are for book reviewers or product reviewers, and the most popular site for these reviews to be posted on is Amazon. You will want to set up two gigs, one for book reviewing and one for product reviews, and you want to focus on Amazon, so you will need an Amazon account to post reviews.

Most of the authors looking for book reviews want the reviews to be verified. A verified review means that you have purchased the book. Don't worry too much yet about buying the book, the customer will reimburse this expense for you.

When I set up the gig, I promise that my reviews will be up to 50 words, this is a target that I can easily hit within a couple of minutes. There is no point in competing on the word length of your reviews. I see Fiverr sellers who promise 300 word reviews; this is serious overkill. Reviews like this don't appear very organic, which is a great way to get Amazon to delete all your reviews. So keep your reviews shorter and try to make your writing appear organic—so don't overthink it.

There a few gig extras that should go with your book reviewer gig. One should be an extra where you agree to post your review on additional sites like Goodreads or Barnes & Noble. Essentially, these additional tasks should take you a couple of minutes to complete. Even at an additional $5, this gig extra has proved very popular. Another gig extra you will need to have is an extra fast option. When you start out your gig, you want to have a delivery time of around 5 to 7 days; this will help you not get too overwhelmed when the orders start flying in. This delay also helps sell your extra fast option of 1 day to buyers. Usually, I charge $10 for the extra fast option. While it is not extremely popular, people do buy it, and that is essentially free money, because it adds nothing to your workload.

The very last gig extra I use is one in which I offer a verified review option. This extra states that I will purchase their book from 99 cents to $3.99. This is another great extra that doesn't add to your workload, and though it is for purchasing the book, you end up making money on this extra. Most authors have their books priced at either 99 cents or $2.99. You get $4 for the gig extra, so you end up pocketing the difference. It's not much, but it can mean that you are making 6 or 7 dollars per gig instead of $4. You'd be surprised how quickly that can add up.

When it comes to my product review gig, I will use only the extra fast option as an extra. Don't bother offering verified reviews as paying for products and wanting for them to be shipped is a hassle. We want to keep our time expenditure short, which means posting quick reviews only without having to wait a week for an item to arrive.

Earlier, I talked about repeat customers and how they are the lifeblood for any Fiverr seller. Well, this is really true when selling reviews; a huge percentage of my orders are from repeat business. This is why it pays to be professional and responsive to your customers.

If you can get a popular review gig on Fiverr, you can make some easy money in very little time. One of my book review gigs was making just over $1000 per month, and it only took me at most forty-five minutes a day to fulfill my orders. While you wouldn't be able to quit your job, it's a nice little bonus for only working forty-five minutes a day.

But to make real money off Fiverr, we are going to have to be able to sell our products for more than five dollars.

The First Fiverr Money-Making Trick

I am now going to get into the real meat of money-making on Fiverr. Over the next three chapters, I will present three product ideas that you will sell to others, but buy on Fiverr. Each of these three ideas can be done separately, or I will show you how to put them all together to maximize your revenue.

Spend your Time Selling

To really make money using Fiverr, you need to concentrate on getting customers and outsourcing the real work to other Fiverrs. This allows you to price your product however you wish. Honestly, we need to make more than the four dollars we get for each Fiverr gig we complete. We need to find customers that will be willing to pay hundreds of dollars for things we can get for five dollars.

Doesn't that sound much more appealing? Let me tell you—it is!

You will remember from the previous chapter how I explained that book review gigs are very popular gigs to start. There is a huge audience for reviews on the Internet. Many of these people and businesses have no idea that Fiverr even exists.

Selling reviews to businesses is the crux of this method. Particularly selling businesses reviews on Yelp. You can use other review sites, but I will concentrate on a system that uses Yelp.

Here is What I Do

The first thing you need to do is get a customer list. Don't worry, it isn't as difficult as it seems. Go to Yelp and essentially go through the businesses, either on Yelp or at the respective website, and get their contact information. It is that easy.

I will then take this list and email them. I have a form letter which offers my services, namely I will provide them with a positive Yelp review for a set price. If the business responds—and you would be surprised at how many do—I will often collect half of the fee up front and the other half on delivery. To make things easier, I use Paypal to complete the transaction.

Once the order has been placed, I then go to Fiverr and hire a gig to complete the review. So if I sell the review for $20, and pay someone to write it for $5, I end up $15 ahead. Not bad, huh?

But this can be better and I will show you how when I explain how to put everything together. The most important thing you can do is build a customer list as you will be using this for all of the methods that I present. The power comes when combining the methods, taking the average package price from a $20 Yelp review to over a hundred dollars.

Making it Work for You

Once you have this general idea down, you can offer reviews for any site. For example, if you want to offer Amazon reviews, you might want to put together your contact list by visiting sites dedicated to writing and writers. Usually targeting customers to build up your list is easy because the groups are easily identifiable and can often be found on the Internet with little effort.

The Second Fiverr Money-Making Trick

The second trick I'm going to present has the same setup as the selling Yelp reviews technique. You will need a customer list of businesses, once again you can get this by researching on Yelp or any other site that provides online business listings.

A Quick Way to Supercharge your List

Honestly, I have never built my own list of contact information for businesses. I have always outsourced this job to a Virtual Assistant. You can hire one for only a few dollars per hour on an outsourcing site like Odesk (http://www.odesk.com), Elance (http://www.elance.com), and even Fiverr has individuals offering to be your Virtual Assistant for a set period of time.

I usually task the assistant with finding business email addresses through a site like Yelp, and usually within a certain city. I like to sort the email addresses to remove any duplicates which I can easily do in Excel, so I suggest having your assistant enter the email addresses in the spreadsheet. Another way of doing it is to enter it in a spreadsheet in Google Docs. For very little money, you can build a fairly comprehensive client list using Virtual Assistants, so I highly recommend it. This will save you time to concentrate on your other ventures.

Putting the Second Trick into Action

The second item we are going to offer to our client list is social media proof. This can be Facebook page likes, Twitter followers or re-tweets, maybe Instagram or Youtube likes. Essentially, we can offer a huge range of social media proof.

There are quite a few sellers that sell real Twitter followers or Facebook likes on Fiverr. Usually they will offer hundreds for five dollars. This is a great place to buy these when you do make a sale.

Be aware that you can also provide the same results by using a social media exchange like Like4Like (http://www.like4like.org). The way a social media exchange works is that you earn credits by liking other people's pages, and then spend those credits when people like your page. You can also pay for credits which might be the easiest method to take depending on how much you are selling the "likes" to your client for.

Understand that when you buy a gig on Fiverr that will give you hundreds of "likes" that these individuals are using a social media service like like4like.org. I want you to know this so you can outsource the job appropriately.

Another option would be to hire a Virtual Assistant to earn the credits through the social media exchange. Whether this is a better solution than paying for the credits either outright or through a Fiverr seller will depend on how much the assistant charges per hour and how many credits they can earn during that time.

To find the method that works best for you will require some experimentation. You may find a great gig on Fiverr that handles everything perfectly. Or you may find that buying the credits saves you the most money and time in the long run. I just wanted to present you with a few different options to help you find the best solution.

How Much Should I Charge?

I have charged some businesses as much as a dollar per "like". However, I suggest over-delivering, if possible. If you can provide 200 "likes" for $50, you will likely have a lot of happy clients. If the demand is high for this package, fiddle with the numbers, just as if the response is tepid, try offering more. Knowing your target is also helpful. Small businesses have less money to spend on this type of marketing, so they will be looking for more bang for their buck. More established businesses may be willing to spend a lot more, however they might be harder to reach someone who can make that decision. The small Mom-and-Pop type businesses are the ones that often gravitate to the services that I offer. This is a good thing to keep in mind when you are deciding on your pricing.

The Third Fiverr Money-Making Trick

The third trick I am going to present once again uses the same setup of the previous two tricks. We are going to use our client list and email them a specific service. In this case, video testimonials.

One of the great gigs that you can buy on Fiverr are video testimonials, with many of them professionally done with ultra-high quality. It is these type of gigs that we are going to want to use.

All of these testimonial gigs will require a script. The best option is to get the business you are doing the testimonial for to write it. But a second option is to outsource the script on Fiverr. You could also obviously write it yourself, but my motto is "never do yourself what you could outsource".

Video testimonials may not be as popular as the other services that you can offer, but they do have one great thing going for them: you can charge quite a bit for them. Especially if they look incredibly professional. And this is why it is important to pick a Fiverr seller who can deliver high definition quality. Because the more professional it looks, the more you can charge your client.

Businesses are convinced that video marketing is expensive, so I play on this fact. Often I will offer a video testimonial for $50 claiming it is deeply discounted. It works.

Another option is to offer to not only provide a video testimonial, but to offer posting it on Youtube and getting it a set amount of views or "likes". Once again, we can accomplish this social media proofing by using a social media exchange or Fiverr seller. This also hints at how we want to put all of these three techniques together. There is a reason we can use all these techniques on a single client list.

What Should I Charge?

I find that offering video testimonials cheaply works extremely well. As I mentioned, people assume that producing video is expensive, so it is fairly easy to offer what most people would consider an inexpensive package. Offering additional views and "likes" for the video also helps tremendously with my sales.

Pricing is one of the factors you really need to play with. I keep track of my conversions and sales for my different pricing levels to see what works best for me. And this is the point: what works best for me might not be what is best for you. How much you can earn is highly dependent on your list. Some lists will outperform others, some will earn more. It is your job to find out what prices work best for your list.

That said, offering video testimonials in the $50 range has always gotten me good responses. Even if you want to offer testimonials for $20, after you pay for the Fiverr gig you still earn $15. Which isn't too bad for being a middleman.

Which Customers Are a Goldmine?

Another thing I would like to point out: treat all your clients with respect and professionalism. It will benefit you in both the short and long run. Repeat customers are an absolute goldmine, so do everything in your power to make certain that all your clients are deliriously happy with the results you provide.

Also, as you get clients make certain you place their contact information on a special clients-only list. This is a great way of targeting previous buyers and offering them special deals.

Putting It All Together

The next step shouldn't be a surprise to anyone. We are going to take all three of the products in the previous chapters and offer them in a single email. Even better, we will offer the products to buy either a la carte or as a package deal.

The trick is to make the package deal the most appealing to the client. You can offer them 2 Yelp reviews, 2 video testimonials and 300 Facebook "likes" for $150, for example. If Yelp reviews cost $20 each, and video testimonials are $50 each, and you offer 100 Facebook "likes" for $50, suddenly the package deal looks fantastic.

I particularly love to play up the savings, advertising things like "this package will get you 20% off the normal price". It is unbelievably effective. And then once you outsource all the work for, say, $25 on Fiverr, you are left with a profit of $125. That's not a bad day's work. With a large enough client list, making thousands of dollars a day is easily within reach even with a low response rate. And as you build up a client list and get repeat customers, your profit can grow and grow.

Taking It to the Next Step

For those who feel comfortable setting up a website, you can always set up a social marketing company website where your potential customers can go. This doesn't have to be a full blown site, it can be as simple as a landing or squeeze page which explains more about your services and attempts to collect more information from the potential client.

If you do have a squeeze page, you can always advertise it on classified sites or even on business related bulletin boards in your signature. Anywhere business owners may be is a great place to mine. Since this is about using Fiverr to make money, I don't want to get too involved in this topic. If you are interested, you can always read an online marketing book which will give you tons of great ideas on how to promote your page.

What Is Good for your Client Is Good for You

Also, don't be shy to use the social media tools that I have given to you, particularly the social media exchange. You can create your social marketing site a Facebook page or a Twitter or Youtube account and get it all the followers and "likes" you want by utilizing the techniques in the previous chapters. This can also be quite helpful if any of your potential clients would like to see an example of your services. It gives you a great amount of social proof.

Using Fiverr to Make Passive Income

The last thing I want to cover is how to use Fiverr to create content that can make you a continuous passive income. There are two areas in which you can get a seller to create content for you that you can repackage and sell passively.

Taking Advantage of a Huge Market

We know that we can get reviews written on Fiverr, but this is only the tip of the iceberg when it comes to writing jobs available on Fiverr. There are many Fiverr sellers offering to write keyword dense content for you for five dollars. Here is how we take advantage of this and turn it into content we can sell.

Electronic books are a huge market online, particularly on Amazon. Now you may think that you need a novel of tens of thousands of words to sell, right? That couldn't be further from the truth. There is a huge market for shorter (think 3000 words or more) non-fiction books. This is the market we want to take advantage of.

We want to decide on a topic, for example, how to lose weight on a low carb diet. We then go to Fiverr and message a seller how much it would cost to get them to write six articles of at least 500 words on this topic. It is pretty easy to find a seller who will do this for around $25. We then package these articles up as an e-book and list it on the Kindle store. Voila, passive income.

There is a whole lot more to Kindle publishing than this, but this is the general idea of how to use Fiverr to create content that can be repackaged and sold elsewhere. If you are interested in publishing Kindle books, I recommend checking out my book, "Kindle Publishing Secrets Revealed", which is an in-depth, step-by-step guide that will teach you how to make money publishing Kindle books.

Getting to the Art of the Matter

Here is another area that you can use to create passive income: illustration. In particular, you want to buy vector illustrations from Fiverr sellers and then repackage them as prints, t-shirts, coffee mugs, and another else that can be printed on.

Here is what you do. I will use Cafepress (http://www.cafepress.com) as an example, but there are other similar sites out there which you can also use. Cafepress allows you to upload your design and then have that design available on a wide array of physical products. Once you upload the design, Cafepress takes care of the rest, including selling, producing, and shipping the products. And you get to collect the check.

This is a fantastic way to earn passive income since you have to do nothing more than commission a design on Fiverr and upload it and decide what products you want your design to appear on at a site like Cafepress.

While both of these methods require an upfront investment, they technically can generate an income for you for years, never requiring any maintenance or updating. It doesn't get much better than that.

Go Forth and Conquer

By employing the tools and techniques that I have taught you in this book, I have no doubt that you will find success.

Also, don't be afraid to add your own twist to your services. New Fiverr gigs are appearing every day, each a potential opportunity to sell more to your business contacts. Always keep an eye on your purpose: to buy services cheaply on Fiverr and sell them for much more to your customer base. With this in mind, you will be shocked with how quickly your bank account can grow.

Good luck, and happy Fiverring!

Preview of "Kindle Publishing Secrets Revealed" by James Chen

Learn to Make Money with Kindle Books

Passive income. We all want to make it. And publishing books on Amazon Kindle is a great way to do it. Imagine your books earning money 24 hours a day, 365 days a year on autopilot, leaving you the time to do whatever you desire. Sounds like a wonderful life, right?

It can be, and the first step is publishing your book. This book will guide you step by step through the process, from initial research to how to market your book.

Don't think you are a very good writer? I will show you how outsource your ideas to other writers who will write the books for you. All you need to do is publish them. And collect the checks.

I will also divulge a secret niche which sees extraordinary sales and searches on Amazon. There are very few writers taking advantage of this trick, and those who have are seeing their books in the bestseller lists. The best part: this niche only requires the books be between 15 to 30 pages in length. Short books, huge rewards.

Learn to take advantage of Amazon's enormous customer base, publishing books that will be searched for, found, and purchased. Learn to get your books to stand out from the millions of other ones already available in the Kindle store. It is simple: if people cannot find your books, they will not buy them. Learn how to be found.

The #1 Rule of Kindle Marketing

The rule is simple: find a process that makes money. And repeat it. Over and over again. This rule is particularly effective in terms of Kindle publishing. You publish your book, market it, let it make money, and do the entire process again.

Too many writers concentrate on one book. They invest all of their energy in making it perfect, trying to build up and audience, instead of writing additional books. Understand that having one book found within millions of books requires a whole lot of luck. But if you have two books, your odds increase. Think of each book as a lottery ticket, the more you have, the more likely you will have one hit the jackpot. Your goal should not be to have one book in the Kindle store, but hundreds. Don't imagine yourself as a writer, but as a publisher. And act accordingly.

Authors often focus on the visible success stories on Amazon, on the fiction writers who have sold hundreds of thousands of books. This is an incredibly small group, and their success is hard to replicate, because it was brought about by luck. You will most likely never get this lucky, so you need to create your own success. That means publishing a lot of books.

The people making money in the system are those who publish hundreds of books under different pen names. These books are often outsourced to a group of writers, as are the formatting and cover creation. This book encourages you to embrace the second method and act like a publisher, producing and selling as much content as you can.

Remember the more you publish, the larger your slice of the pie will be.

I hope you enjoyed the free preview of "Kindle Publishing Secrets Revealed" by James Chen.

Click here to check out the rest of Kindle Publishing Secrets Revealed on Amazon.

Or go to:

http://www.amazon.com/dp/B00K5I3MC0/

Preview of "Essential Oils" by Emily V. Steinhauser

Essential Oils

Essential oils are oils that are extracted from the flowers, leaves, fruits, peel, seeds, woods, bark, roots, and other natural materials. There are thousands of different kinds of essential oils, and each has unique properties and characteristics. They are highly volatile so they are easily absorbed by the skin. So one wants to take care in the use of them.

Many body care products contain essential oils that they use for their therapeutic properties, and not just for their scent. There are many essential oils that are an effective treatment for a number of different skin conditions. They are extremely concentrated and powerful. They can be regenerative both in physical and emotional ways, making you feel healthy and stronger. The benefits cannot be understated, essential oils can have a dramatic impact on how you look and feel.

This book will explore the various ways that one can use essential oils. I will also present the best oils to use in each specific situation, both from research and personal experience. Sections will focus on the using essential oils to treat, heal, and rejuvenate one's skin. We will also explore how to use essential oils to thicken one's hair, promote faster hair re-growth, and how to deal with hair loss.

Essential oils are often used therapeutically, and I will talk about the medicinal uses of essential oils. I will not only focus on physical application of the oils, but also on aromatherapy and the benefits it provides.

One of my favorite uses of essential oils is using them to deal with headaches, including migraines. They also prove efficacious for first aid, particularly in the reduction of swelling and the healing of bruises. I will also present information on how you can use essential oils to sharpen your mental focus, improve your concentration, and enhance your overall memory.

I am excited that you have joined me on this journey through the essential oils. I hope they bring you a long lifetime of improved health and comfort.

I hope you enjoyed the free preview of "Essential Oils" by Emily V. Steinhauser.

Click here to check out the rest of Essential Oils by Emily V. Steinhauser on Amazon.

Or go to:

http://www.amazon.com/dp/B00KD4CD0I

Other Books Available From Gamma Mouse Media

Below you will find other popular Amazon bestsellers from Gamma Mouse Media. Simply click on the links to check them out.

Essential Oils – Emily V. Steinhauser

Forex Indicators – Warren R. Sullivan

Kindle Publishing Secrets Revealed – James Chen

Procrastination – Warren R. Sullivan

Brain Training Boot Camp – Warren R. Sullivan

Knee Pain Treatment – Emily V. Steinhauser

Marriage Problems – Emily V. Steinhauser

Quiet – Amelia Austin

Lust for Me – Amelia Austin

Cellulite Reduction – Emily V. Steinhauser

The Quick Start Guide to Macarons – Lindsay Stotts

Speed Reading Training – Warren R. Sullivan

Memory Enhancement – Warren R. Sullivan

The Quick Start Guide to Perfect Pancakes – Lindsay Stotts

Compulsive Hoarding – Emily V. Steinhauser

If the links above do not work, you can simply search for these titles on Amazon's website to find them.

www.ingramcontent.com/pod-product-compliance
Lightning Source LLC
Chambersburg PA
CBHW071647170526
45166CB00003B/1474